FEED YOUR HEAD

REDISCOVERING PSYCHEDELIC MEDICINE

BY GARY MCGREW

For every person who struggles with a mental health condition. We are just beginning to understand the options nature has to offer in helping us feel like ourselves again. I hope you find this book to be informative, helpful and hopeful. Remember, you are not alone.

DISCLAIMER

The laws and regulations regarding psilocybin mushrooms vary greatly depending on where you live in the world. Many places have stringent laws prohibiting not just the recreational use of psychedelics, but also their cultivation and possession. If considering use of psilocybin mushrooms in any capacity, research your local laws and regulations first to understand the legal risks involved. While an interesting area of study, recreational use, microdosing or growing psychedelics may carry serious legal consequences depending on your jurisdiction.

Proceed with abundant caution and legal awareness.

The contents of this document should not be taken as legal or medical advice.

TABLE OF CONTENTS

CHAPTER 1

Tracing the Evolutionary History of Mushrooms and Humans

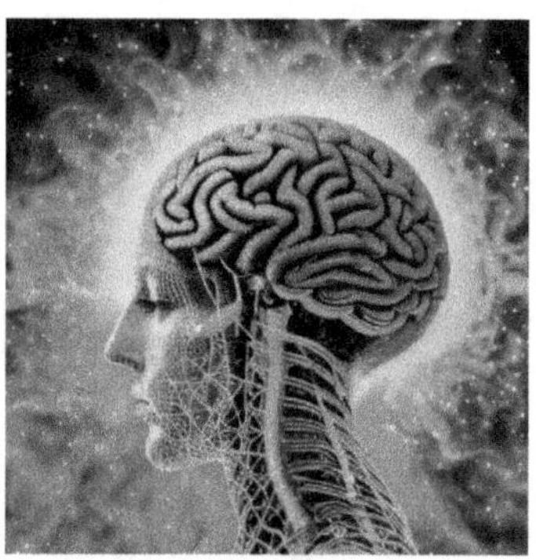

Mushrooms have an incredibly ancient lineage, with fossil evidence showing mushroom-forming fungi dating back over 100 million years. Though humans have only been around for about 6 million years, mushrooms and humans have co-evolved and influenced each other in fascinating ways.

Mushrooms are part of the fungi kingdom, a distinct branch of life separate from plants and animals. Fungi are more closely related to animals than plants, and share some common ancestors with humans. In particular, fungi and animals both digest food externally and store carbohydrates in the form of glycogen.

One key evolutionary milestone for fungi was the development of mycelium - a vast underground web of root-like filaments that absorb nutrients. Mycelium allowed fungi to spread, exchange nutrients and interact with plant roots. This symbiosis between mycelium and plant roots played a crucial role in enabling plants to colonize land.

Around 140-110 million years ago, the first mushroom forming fungi emerged. Mushrooms are the reproductive structures of certain fungi that develop above ground or on food sources to release spores. These reproductively complex fungi probably evolved along with insects, using wind and insect dispersal to spread spores far and wide.

One major evolutionary leap was the development of mycorrhizal relationships between fungi and plant roots. Mycorrhizal fungi supply plants with water and nutrients in exchange for sugars produced by photosynthesis. This mutually beneficial relationship likely enabled early land plants to thrive and grow larger.

Homo sapiens evolved roughly 300,000 years ago. As early humans spread around the globe, we learned to take advantage of mushrooms in diverse ways. Nearly every human culture utilizes wild mushrooms as food and medicine. Mushrooms became engrained in cultural stories and myths. The co-evolutionary relationship between humans and fungi was further cultivated once we learned to grow mushrooms intentionally.

Modern genetic analysis reveals that humans share a subset of disease-fighting genes with fungi. This implies a long co-evolutionary history of fighting similar pathogens. Fungi have also evolved genes similar to those that regulate sleep and circadian rhythms in humans. This biological kinship reflects the intertwined evolutionary fates of our two kingdoms.

While humans and mushrooms have followed very different evolutionary paths, we remain connected through a web of complex biological and ecological relationships. As we learn more, it becomes clear just how influential fungi have been throughout Earth's history and in shaping the trajectory of human civilization.

CHAPTER 2

Exploring the Ancient and Mysteries of Psychedelics

The use of psychedelic plants and fungi for spiritual, medicinal and cultural purposes stretches back thousands of years, long before concepts like "drugs" or "psychedelics" entered the modern lexicon. By examining archaeological evidence and practices in indigenous cultures, we can trace the captivating history of these consciousness-altering substances.

Perhaps the most well-known psychedelic used in ancient times is the psilocybin mushroom. Indigenous peoples across the world have cultivated a deep spiritual relationship with these mushrooms for millennia. Remnants of psychedelic mushrooms have been found in cave paintings dating back over 9,000 years in Algeria. Ancient artworks from Central and South American cultures like the Aztec, Maya, Zapotec and Moche depict psychedelic mushrooms.

The Aztecs in particular revered teonanácatl, meaning "god's flesh," as a sacrament and key to enlightenment.

Here's a fun fact: The Aztec's reverence for psychedelic mushrooms was so intense that they prohibited commoners from taking them, reserving mushrooms only for high priests and nobility. Breaking this ancient drug law could be punishable by death!

Clear evidence for ritualistic drinking of psychedelic mushroom potions has been found in well-preserved artifacts and mummies from indigenous Andean shamans.

Carbon dating traces some of this sacred mushroom use to 1000-2000 BCE. Similarly, archaeological finds in Guatemala from 1000-500 BCE contain unmistakable mushroom effigies, indicating their cultural significance.

These practices were not limited to the Americas either. Siberian shamans have long consumed the psychedelic Amanita muscaria mushrooms to achieve trance states. Remarkably, rock art in the Sahara dated between 7000 and 9000 years ago depicts mushroom-like symbols. This implies humans engaged with psilocybin far earlier than many imagined.

Here's a wild fact: There's a conspiracy theory that the vivid red and white colors of the Amanita muscaria mushroom inspired the iconic look of Santa Claus! The story goes that shamans would collect these hallucinogenic fungi and climb down chimneys to leave them as presents.

While indigenous use of psychedelics is well-documented, there remains debate around how these cultures first discovered these substances. Some fringe theories suggest psilocybin mushrooms first arrived on meteorites. While mushrooms do have some extraterrestrial connections – a few species have been found growing on the International Space Station!

More likely is that early humans experimented with various plants and fungi, slowly learning which induced altered states of consciousness spiritually prized by ancient societies. Trial and error over many generations allowed indigenous peoples across the world to independently develop rich spiritual traditions around psychedelics.

Their influence on both culture and consciousness cannot be overstated. The long history of psychedelic usage stands in stark contrast to their prohibition under modern drug laws. Looking back on how mushrooms, ayahuasca, peyote and other substances were woven into the very fabric of diverse ancient societies highlights the complex relationship humans have long had with these plants and fungi.

Only now are we beginning to rediscover the profound lessons psychedelics have to teach us, after a brief interlude of denial. With an open and curious mindset, modern science is beginning to tap into psychedelics' vast therapeutic and spiritual potential, much like our ancestors did millennia ago.

CHAPTER 3

The Long, Strange Trip of Psychedelic Criminalization

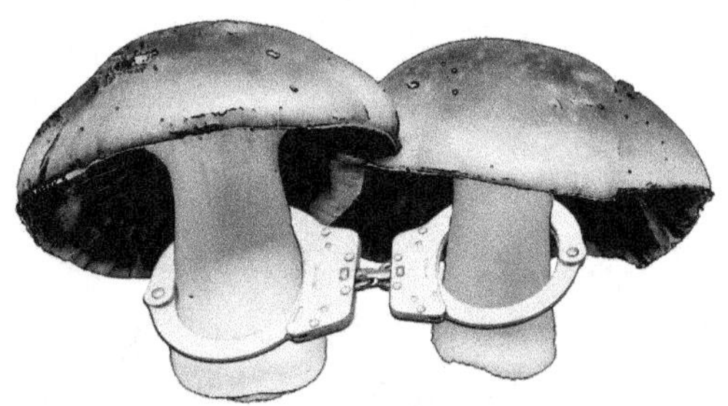

Psychedelics like LSD, psilocybin and mescaline were once considered wonder drugs by psychiatry in the 1950s-60s for their potential to treat addiction, anxiety and more. But a mix of fear, politics and hype led to these compounds being branded as dangerous, ending promising research prematurely.

In the 1950s, psychedelics burst onto the psychiatric scene as researchers discovered these compounds had remarkable effects on consciousness. Scientists like Timothy Leary conducted experiments showing how LSD could benefit addiction treatment and improve mood in cancer patients.

By the early 1960s, there were over 1000 scientific papers on the therapeutic potential of psychedelics. The US government even funded studies, with the FDA approving new uses. At conferences like the 1964 American Psychiatric Association annual meeting, over 40% of presentations covered psychedelic science.

However, recreational use of psychedelics also exploded in the 1960s counterculture movement. Timothy Leary infamously advocated using psychedelics to "Turn on, tune in, drop out". This evangelizing alarmed the establishment. As one humorous example, the FBI under J. Edgar Hoover once labelled Leary "the most dangerous man in America".

The final nail in the coffin was the 1970 Controlled Substances Act. President Nixon, who labelled Leary as "an extremely dangerous man," signed the act which placed strict limits on psychedelics. This was heavily influenced by figures like Harry J. Anslinger who used propaganda and misinformation in his war on drugs.

The Schedule I status had immediate effects on research. Funding evaporated almost overnight, with psychedelic projects shut down. Possession of substances like LSD and psilocybin became serious felonies. Experts argue this pushed psychedelics into the black market and culture of crime.

After 50 years, the tide is finally turning on the thoughtless criminalization of psychedelics. A new wave of research from top universities has demonstrated benefits for mental health. Groups like MAPS are funding large-scale clinical trials aimed at medical approval. Legally, compounds like psilocybin are being decriminalized in certain cities and states.

While psychedelics clearly have risks requiring regulation, their blanket criminalization has prevented huge therapeutic potential from being realized. As we undo past excesses, perhaps these compounds can improve wellbeing when used judiciously with qualified support. Their long, strange trip in law may finally be headed in a rational direction.

CHAPTER 4

The Promise and Potential of Psychedelic Microdosing

Microdosing, the practice of regularly taking very low doses of psychedelics like LSD or psilocybin, has surged in popularity in recent years. Though not inducing full-blown trips, a growing body of anecdotal reports and preliminary research suggests potential cognitive and emotional benefits from microdosing.

One of the most widely reported effects of microdosing is improved focus, productivity and creativity. Software developers in Silicon Valley helped popularize the practice, claiming tiny doses of LSD allow them to stay focused on complex coding for hours. Lab experiments also indicate psychedelic microdoses enhance some markers of fluid intelligence and cognitive flexibility. A study from Imperial College London found participants solved problems more quickly after microdosing LSD. Enhanced creativity and outside-the-box thinking are also commonly reported in surveys of microdosers.

Clinical research remains limited but initial results are promising.

A groundbreaking study from Imperial College London in 2019 found significant reductions in reported depression among participants who microdosed psilocybin truffles for several weeks, compared to a placebo group. At the University of Toronto, microdosing psilocybin also decreased symptoms of anxiety and depression. Neuroimaging shows psychedelics stimulate growth of new connections in brain regions linked to emotional processing and social cognition. This may allow microdosers to break negative thought patterns and view situations through a more positive lens.

While placebo-controlled trials are still needed, hundreds of anecdotal reports indicate better mood, focus, sociability, and well-being on dosing days. Rogue pharmacologist James Fadiman, who conducted pioneering microdosing studies, claims it can have profound impacts on work and relationships when combined with journaling about experiences. However, some users report no effects from microdosing, or find benefits fade over time. Dosing amount and frequency can also take trial-and-error to optimize. Starting low and tracking effects seem to be key.

With responsible use and more research, microdosing could pave the way for tapping psychedelics' therapeutic potential without drastic perception changes. Margaret, a 50 year old with anxiety, sums up her microdosing experience: "It's not a magic happy pill, but it gives me more capacity to handle challenges. My mind feels more expansive." While uncertainties remain, psychedelic microdosing shows promising psychological benefits meriting serious scientific inquiry.

While most research has involved LSD, many people microdose with psilocybin mushrooms instead. Psilocybin is the main psychoactive compound in over 200 species of mushrooms, including the commonly microdosed Psilocybe cubensis. Anecdotal reports suggest mushrooms provide similar benefits to microdosed LSD, with less risk of anxiety or overstimulation.

Psilocybin microdoses are typically around 0.1 to 0.5 grams of dried mushrooms. At this low level, there are no perceptible psychedelic effects. However, some users report mood boosting after-effects that last for days. One study found microdosing mushrooms improved feelings of vitality, gratitude and focus on dosing days.

Psilocybin may be particularly therapeutic for those struggling with anxious rumination, obsessive thoughts or pessimism. Even microdoses appear to reduce excessive activity in the brain's default mode network, associated with being trapped in thought loops. This can allow for more presence, flexibility and optimism.

Microdosing mushrooms could also benefit creatives who feel stuck or uninspired. Many artists, musicians and writers report entering immersive flow states after psilocybin microdoses. By adding neurological noise, microdoses may jolt one out of rigid thought patterns into expansive ideation. The effects tend to be subtle compared to full doses, enabling industrious creativity.

It's important to note psilocybin microdosing affects everyone differently. For some it may increase anxiety, especially in already stressful times. Those predisposed to psychosis should avoid microdosing too. Starting with tiny doses and self-observation days is recommended to assess how you respond.

Used judiciously, microdosing mushrooms shows promise for improving wellbeing, focus, creativity and flexibility. More clinical trials are underway, but early findings and self-experiments suggest potentials meriting cautious exploration. As with any psychedelic, having clear intentions and integrating experiences is key to maximizing benefits.

CHAPTER 5

Exploring Psychedelic Macrodosing and its Revelations

While microdosing involves small doses, macrodosing means taking a full psychedelic trip dose. Though intense, proponents argue macrodosing in proper contexts can induce profound changes in perspectives and priorities.

The comedian Russell Brand has publicly discussed his recreational experiences macrodosing psilocybin mushrooms in his youth, describing vivid hallucinations of furniture and wallpaper coming to life. While he found it exhilarating initially, Brand warns macrodosing can also invite terrifying sensory distortions if not approached carefully.

The author Michael Pollan famously experimented with macrodosing LSD and mushrooms while researching his book on psychedelics. He felt his ego temporarily dissolve as his normal sense of self melted away. While disorienting, Pollan says the experience granted him fresh clarity on his relationships and the arbitrary ways we segment time into artificial milestones.

The actress Kristen Bell has also spoken openly about therapeutically macrodosing mushrooms under guidance to treat her depression and anxiety. She said the experience elicited deep emotional breakthroughs and honest evaluation of patterns in her life. While challenging, Bell says she emerged with greater self-knowledge and lasting relief from racing thoughts.

However, without proper support, macrodosing can go sideways. The podcaster Joe Rogan has described unsettling experiences watching friends macrodose recklessly in chaotic party contexts. He cautions taking psychedelics solely for recreation, saying important insights can be missed without thoughtful integration. Proper set and setting radically decrease risks.

Research confirms guided macrodoses can induce lasting personality changes by profoundly shaking up perspectives. One study showed macrodosing increased openness, nature relatedness and cognitive flexibility when paired with talk therapy. While intoxicating short-term, psychedelics may catalyze post-traumatic growth when approached wisely.

While psilocybin is the main psychoactive compound, different mushroom species and strains produce noticeably different experiences when macrodosed.

Psilocybe cubensis is the most common magic mushroom used both for micro and macrodoses. Their effects are considered classic and representative of the psilocybin experience. At higher doses, P. cubensis delivers strong visual hallucinations, euphoria and sense of childlike wonder. However, some also report periods of anxiety and self-consciousness mid-trip on cubensis.

Psilocybe azurescens contains up to 1.8% psilocybin, giving it a strong, spiritually-oriented high. The visionary effects are powerful, with increased chances of out-of-body sensations or mystical states compared to other varieties. However, the body load can be taxing, with considerable nausea lasting hours.

Conversely, Psilocybe tampanensis provides a lighter, more playful trip. Known as the "philosopher's stone" mushroom, tampanensis induces deep reflective thinking and heightened creativity without being too heavy. Users describe laughing fits, cartoonish visuals and youthful giddiness when macrodosing tampanensis.

For those seeking visual intensity, Psilocybe mexicana could be ideal. The hallucinatory trip tends to be very lively and lucid. Closed-eye visuals on P. mexicana have an electric, dreamlike quality compared to other mushrooms. However, the comedown can be sharp with sudden mood drops.

Always approach macrodoses with care and intention-setting, regardless of species. Dosage, mindset and environment modulate the experience as much as variety of mushroom. Responsible macrodosing requires an experienced guide to maximize revelation while minimizing potential psychic risks.

CHAPTER 6

Psilocybe Cubensis and its Many Magical Guises

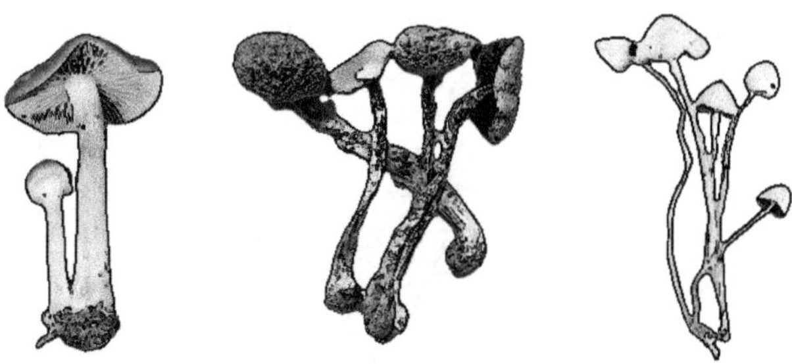

Psilocybe cubensis is the most well-known and widely used species of psychedelic mushroom. Within P. cubensis there are dozens of different strains and varieties, each with unique aesthetics, potency, and reported effects.

One of the most popular is Golden Teacher, named for its golden caps. It is a classic mushroom known for its philosophical, spiritual insights. Golden Teacher delivers a warm, reflective experience with strong closed eye visuals and a moderately powerful body high.

B+ mushrooms have a dark brown cap and thick white stems. They are considered reliable mood enhancers that provide a gentle, loving perspective. B+ is very beginner friendly though may be underwhelming for experienced trippers. The come-up and comedown tend to be gradual and smooth.

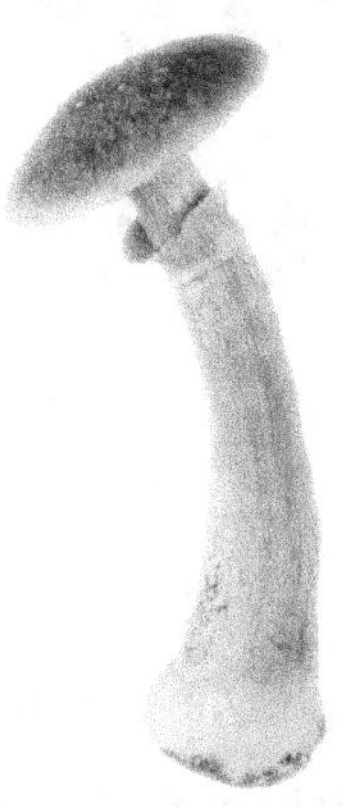

Looking distinct with long, slender stems, Penis Envy shrooms are more potent than average P. cubensis. The visual effects are more neon and interactive, with greater aphrodisiac qualities compared to others. But Penis Envy may produce muscle tension and restlessness at intense doses.

Whatever your needs, there exists a P. cubensis variety well-suited to provide a quality trip. As with any mushroom, potency and individual reactions vary. Starting slow and paying attention to your body and mind will allow you to safely experience all these unique cubes have to offer.

Growing Your Own Medicinal Mushrooms

With the recent surge in interest around the health benefits of functional mushrooms like reishi, lion's mane and turkey tail, many people are looking into growing mushrooms at home for their personal use. Growing mushrooms does require some initial investment and learning, but can be done with relative ease once the basic techniques are understood. Here is an overview of what's needed and how to get started with a home mushroom cultivation project.

Supplies Needed

- Pressure cooker or pot with lid to sterilize substrates
- Inoculation tools - syringe, loops, etc to transfer mushroom mycelium
- Containers for substrates such as jars, bags or plastic boxes

- Growing substrates like grain, wood chips or coffee grounds
- Perlite, vermiculite or other casing materials
- Humidity tent or Martha grow tent with humidifier and air system
- Thermometer for monitoring conditions
- Fans or other airflow system
- Spores or liquid cultures for desired mushroom strains

Inoculating Grains and Substrates

Once you have your supplies and spores or cultures, you can begin preparing your substrates for mushroom growth. Sterilize all containers and tools first to prevent contamination. Grains like rye, rice or millet are commonly used and hydrated first before sterilizing. Once cooled, use a syringe to inoculate with spores following sterile procedures.

Other substrates like coffee, wood chips or straw can also be inoculated. Place lids on containers and store in a climate controlled area around 75F. Within a couple weeks, you should see white, threadlike mycelium start to spread across the substrates, signaling growth.

Fruiting and Maintenance

When the substrates are fully colonized by mushroom mycelium, introduce to a humid, controlled environment to induce fruiting. Cakes can be birthed from jars dunked in water and rolled in vermiculite. Bulk substrates are typically layered with more vermiculite and casing. Maintaining humidity around 95%, temperatures between 68-75F and regular air exchange will support optimum mushroom formation.

The entire process from inoculation to fruiting can take 6-12 weeks depending on factors like strain, substrates and growing conditions. Proper maintenance is key - be sure to fan and mist tanks daily, watch for any contamination and make adjustments to dial in the microclimate. With some patience you'll start harvesting homegrown medicinal mushrooms!

Levels of Difficulty

For beginners, starting with a PF-Tek style grow using pre-sterilized mushroom substrate cakes is recommended. This allows you to get the basics of inoculation and fruiting. However, cake grows produce lower yields.

Another option is using an all-in-one grow bag, which comes pre-filled with sterilized substrate. Simply inject the spore syringe or liquid culture into the inoculation port. The bags have built-in microfiltration patches to allow gas exchange while blocking contaminants. All-in-one bags provide an easy way to grow mushrooms with less equipment and preparation required.

For larger, continual harvests, monotub grows with bulk substrates like manure composts can support canopy flushes but require more equipment and steps like pasteurization. Partnering with an experienced grower helps shorten the learning curve considerably.

Preventing Contamination

When cultivating mushrooms at home, maintaining sterile conditions is critical to prevent contamination from mold, bacteria and other microbes. Ensure all equipment and substrates are sterilized properly before inoculation. Work in a clean environment using gloves and alcohol to sanitize.

Look for any unusual colors, odors or textures on the mushroom substrates, which likely signals contamination. Trichoderma green mold and cobweb mold are common culprits. Isolate any contaminated bags or jars immediately to prevent spreading spores. Learn proper sterile technique and continue fine-tuning your grow area to limit risks of contamination.

With adequate space and some supplies, mushrooms can be cultivated at home to reap their unique health benefits. Follow sterile procedures closely and fine-tune humidity, FAE and temperatures for your mushroom strains. Then you'll be on your way to a thriving medicinal mushroom operation.

EPILOGUE

We have co-existed and co-evolved with fungi for eons, shaping ecosystems and civilizations. Psychedelics hint at untapped fungal mysteries still to be unraveled through science. Even growing mushrooms at home perpetuates an age-old bond, symbiotically exchanging nutrients and knowledge.

As our understanding of fungi grows, so does our awe at nature's ingenuity. Mushrooms offer inspirational lessons about cooperation, healing, consciousness and sustainability that we would be wise to integrate. If humanity listens and learns, fungi may guide us to wiser, healthier futures for all earthlings, human and mushroom alike.

Our shared fungal heritage is a reminder that, despite surface differences, all organisms are interconnected in the great web of life. As we rediscover ancient bonds with mushrooms, we may also rediscover who we are and why we are here - fellow travelers on a psychedelic planet hurtling through space and time.

www.ingramcontent.com/pod-product-compliance
Lightning Source LLC
Chambersburg PA
CBHW060820260726

48660CB00003B/1025